Kids in Sports

A CHAPTER BOOK

BY KIRSTEN HALL

children's press ®

A Division of Scholastic Inc.
New York   Toronto   London   Auckland   Sydney
Mexico City   New Delhi   Hong Kong
Danbury, Connecticut

For Tiffany Kim, who likes to think she's lazy
but is actually quite a little athlete!

ACKNOWLEDGMENTS

The author would like to thank Rudy Garcia-Tolson, Grant Paulsen,
and Gavonnah Williams for their help in making this book happen.
Despite their busy schedules, they were extremely generous with their time.
They are, indeed, true superstars.

Library of Congress Cataloging-in-Publication Data

Hall, Kirsten.
  Kids in sports : a chapter book / by Kirsten Hall.
    p. cm. – (True tales)
Includes bibliographical references and index.
  ISBN 0-516-23733-0 (Lib. Bdg.)   0-516-24685-2 (pbk.)
  1. Sports–Biography–Juvenile literature. 2. Children–Biography–Juvenile literature.
  I. Title. II. Series.

GV697.A1H33 2004
796'.092'2–dc22

                        2004000425

CONTENTS

INTRODUCTION

Believe it or not, some of the greatest athletes of all time have been children. You are about to read about four young people who played an important role in sports. Each one has proven that kids can do things just as well as adults, and sometimes even better!

Nadia Comaneci made history when she scored the first perfect ten in **gymnastics** (jim-NASS-tiks). Rudy Garcia-Tolsen was told he might spend his life in a wheelchair. Today he is a record-breaking **triathlete** (trye-ATH-leet). Gavonnah Williams's **karate** (kah-RAH-tee) moves were so advanced that he wasn't allowed to use them. Grant Paulsen interviews professional athletes.

Success didn't fall into the hands of these four kids. They worked hard at being the best. After all, it's not always easy to be taken seriously when you are young. What these kids knew is that the world of sports isn't just a place for adults, it's for kids, too!

CHAPTER ONE

RAISING THE BAR

Montreal, Canada, was the proud host of the 1976 Summer **Olympic Games**. Inside the arena of the Montreal Forum, people cheered loudly for their favorite athletes. Lost in the crowd of **gymnasts** was a little girl from **Romania** named Nadia Comaneci. Few people in the audience even knew her name.

At fourteen years of age, she was tiny, just under 5 feet (1.5 meters) tall and 86 pounds (39 kilograms). As the other gymnasts performed around her, no one even looked Nadia's way.

Nadia Comaneci

Nadia performs on the uneven bars.

Nadia had no idea that her life was about to change. When it was her turn on the **uneven bars**, Nadia grabbed hold of a bar with both hands and began to swing. Up and down, back and forth, Nadia swung gracefully from one bar to the other.

Nadia in front of the scoreboard

Her movements were quick and beautiful to watch.

The crowds buzzed with questions. Who was she? Where had she come from? Why hadn't anyone seen her before? When Nadia landed on the ground at the end of her **routine** (roo-TEEN), she bowed for the audience. As she walked off the floor, her teammates watched her, speechless. They knew Nadia was about to get a top score.

Moments later, Nadia's score flashed on the scoreboard. The number was 1.00. Nadia knew that the judges scored on a scale of one to ten. A one was not a very good score at all.

Then the crowd began to cheer. Thousands of hands clapped in her honor. Only then did Nadia realize what was happening. The scoreboard hadn't been set up to record anything higher than 9.99.

She hadn't scored 1.00. She had scored 10.00, a perfect score! Nadia had the first perfect ten in Olympic history!

Nadia wears one of her three gold medals.

Nadia went on to earn six more perfect scores. By the end of the Olympics, she had won three gold medals, one silver medal, and one bronze.

Fourteen years before the Montreal Olympics, on November 12, 1961, Nadia Comaneci was born. She grew up in Romania, a country in southeastern Europe, in a small apartment with her father, Gheorghe, her mother, Alexandrina, and her younger brother, Adrian.

Even as a small child, Nadia was an excellent athlete. She had lots of energy and loved to compete. In school, she and her best friend enjoyed playing soccer with the boys. The boys were often disappointed because the girls often won.

One day two coaches came to Nadia's school. Bela Karolyi and his wife, Marta, watched the children play in the school yard. The coaches were hoping to find some girls to join their gymnastics school. Two schoolgirls stood out as being very good. One of the girls was Nadia.

Bela and Marta Karolyi, Nadia's coaches, with another young gymnast

When the school bell rang, the two girls disappeared into their classroom. The Karolyis checked each classroom, but they didn't see them anywhere. The couple decided to walk through each of the classrooms once more before leaving. As they entered each room, they asked, "Who loves gymnastics?" Finally, they found the two girls they had been looking for. "It is we!" Nadia called back to them.

From that day forward, Nadia's life became gymnastics. With her parents' approval, she joined the Karolyis's gymnastics school. There was a lot that Nadia was going to need to learn. The Karolyis were pleased to find that Nadia was an eager student.

Nadia's training was hard work. She spent four hours every day in the gym. Each time she learned a new move, her coaches would hold her body to show her what it would feel like.

Nadia does a back handspring on the balance beam.

Then she would try to do the move on her own. Nadia practiced these moves again and again until she could do them perfectly.

At the school, Nadia's life was very different. Her friends were all gymnasts. Her food was specially chosen for her. She and the other gymnasts even had their own doctor. Nadia had all the support she needed to be a star.

Winning the first perfect score in the history of the Olympics was an amazing moment in Nadia's life. For several more years, Nadia continued to compete, winning many more competitions.

In 1980, the Olympics felt very different to Nadia. She was no longer an unknown gymnast. Now she was the one everyone else wanted to beat. She didn't feel very well at the time of the games. Her legs bothered her terribly.

The crowd gasped when Nadia missed one of the easiest moves on the bars and landed on the floor. Even though Nadia ended up winning two gold medals and two silver medals that year, people no longer saw her as perfect. Nadia realized that she didn't like the pressure of having to be perfect. Her dreams were no longer her own, they were everyone's.

Four years later, Nadia retired from gymnastics. She decided she would rather judge competitions than be in them. She also went on to coach children. Today, Nadia and her husband, Bart Conner, run a large gymnastics school in Norman, Oklahoma.

Nadia and Bart Conner

A grown-up Nadia poses with young gymnasts.

CHAPTER TWO

PROVING THEM WRONG

As the finish line came into view, ten-year-old Rudy Garcia-Tolson searched the crowd for his mother. He smiled when he found her. She was clapping and cheering him on. Rudy is a **double amputee.** Five years earlier, both his legs had been cut off in an operation. Rudy did not let this stop him from doing what he wanted to do. With a few more steps, he crossed the finish line and completed his first **triathlon** (trye-ATH-lon).

His father hugged him and congratulated him. The crowd's cheers were so loud that Rudy could hardly hear his father's words.

Rudy Garcia-Tolson

Rudy was born with **Pterygium Syndrome**, a very rare condition. When he was born both of his hands were webbed. One of his feet twisted in toward the other. The doctors told Rudy's parents that he would probably never walk.

Rudy spent the first five years of his life feeling lonely. After fifteen operations, he had to stay in a wheelchair. Most days he sat by his window and watched the other kids play. He wished he could be like them.

Rudy and his parents talked to their doctors. The doctors gave the family two choices. Rudy could have his legs **amputated** at the knees and be fitted with special legs. If he didn't, he would spend the rest of his life in a wheelchair.

Rudy's parents let Rudy decide. Rudy was scared. What if he had both of his legs amputated and he still couldn't walk? What if he made the wrong decision?

In the end, Rudy chose to have the operation because he wanted to be "just like the other kids."

In many ways, Rudy is now just like other kids. He goes to school, spends time with his friends, and plays on his computer.

Rudy doesn't need his special legs to swim.

Rudy skateboarding

However, Rudy is also different from other boys his age. Rudy wears a **prosthesis** (pross-THEE-siss) on each leg. Rudy's new legs are made out of foam and carbon fiber. He has different sets of legs for different activities.

At first, Rudy didn't like his special legs. They often broke. It was hard for him to ride his bicycle or run. Even walking was difficult.

Now Rudy likes his special legs. They are better quality. They don't break. Rudy can do anything with them. He runs races, bikes, and even climbs mountains.

One day Rudy met Terry Martin, a fellow athlete. Terry asked Rudy to be his partner in an upcoming triathlon. Rudy and Terry beat all of the other teams in the competition. At the awards ceremony, Terry held Rudy up for everyone in the audience to see. The cheers seemed to last forever. Rudy was a hero.

Rudy loved competing in triathlons. He started with short distances and worked his way up to longer races. Soon Rudy became popular. He was thrilled when stars like

Rudy uses his special legs to ride a bike.

Sean Astin and Robin Williams asked to be his partner in triathlons.

Rudy's mother says that Rudy has opened the door for other challenged athletes. Rudy's father says that he has proven that challenged kids can do anything other kids can do.

"When I first started running, there were no races for double amputees. People didn't think we could do it. But now, I'm proving them wrong. I want to show **disabled** (diss-AY-buhld) kids that it's worth coming out and competing," says Rudy.

Indeed, it is. Twice in the last ten years, Rudy has been named "Challenged Athlete of the Year." He is the youngest double amputee to ever complete a triathlon on his own. In 2002, Rudy was chosen to carry the torch at the Winter Olympics.

In 2003, *Teen People* magazine called Rudy one of "20 Teens Who Will Change the World." With any luck, the magazine's **prediction** will come true. After all, the world could use a hero like Rudy.

Rudy carries the torch in the 2002 Winter Olympics.

CHAPTER THREE

CHANGING THE RULES

At a karate tournament in Florida, Gavonnah Williams felt relaxed and sure of himself. Herbie Williams, Gavonnah's father and coach, saw that his six-year-old son was confident. That meant Gavonnah was likely to win. Right before the competition started, however, one of the **officials** (uh-FISH-uhls) came over to Herbie and Gavonnah. The official told them that Gavonnah wouldn't be allowed to compete that day.

Gavonnah Williams

Gavonnah's **techniques** (tek-NEEKS) were too advanced. He was using moves that other six-year-olds didn't know yet.

"Why should Gavonnah be punished for the fact that he's better than the others?" Herbie demanded. The official said he was sorry, but there was nothing he could do.

Gavonnah felt sad. His mother, Annie, tried to comfort him. She said, "Don't let them get you down. We won't go backward. We will only go forward." Gavonnah hoped she was right. He had come so far. He didn't want to stop competing.

Gavonnah began learning karate when he was three years old. Back then, his mother thought he was too shy. She hoped that learning karate would give him confidence.

From the beginning, Gavonnah loved karate. He began spending almost all of his time outside of school training to be the best he could be. That hard work continues today.

Every day Gavonnah puts on a **gi** (GEE), his karate outfit. Gavonnah wears a pair of loose pants and a comfortable cotton jacket. He ties his jacket closed with a black belt. Only experts can wear black belts.

Gavonnah performing his advanced moves

Gavonnah ties the black belt to his gi.

Gavonnah practices for two hours every day in a **dojo** (DOH-joh). He practices with other children. First they stretch. Then they pound their hands and feet on padded boards. Doing this helps their hands and feet get tough.

Sometimes the students practice together. Other times they pretend they have **opponents**. When they practice fighting against one another, they must be careful. They are only allowed to touch each other lightly. They must follow the rules of karate. One important rule is that a person can use full force only when defending oneself.

The students in Gavonnah's dojo practice five different types of techniques. They practice different ways of standing, called stances. They learn to defend themselves by blocking an opponent's moves. They also study different ways of kicking, punching, and striking.

There are two kinds of karate competitions. In form competitions, Gavonnah performs his techniques alone before a panel of judges. Each judge gives him a score from one to ten. In free fighting competitions, Gavonnah fights against an opponent. He does not prepare his moves beforehand.

Gavonnah leads a karate class.

It's not surprising that Gavonnah enjoys competitions. After all, he does so well in them. Today, at the age of nine, Gavonnah has nearly 150 awards and trophies. He has competed in North and South America, Europe, and Asia.

Gavonnah's proudest moment in karate did not happen when he was traveling around the world. It took place right in his home state of Florida. It didn't involve winning a competition. Instead, it was about changing the rules.

Karate judges had ruled that some of Gavonnah's **aerial** (AIR-ee-uhl) kicks were **illegal**. They argued that because other kids couldn't do the moves, Gavonnah shouldn't be allowed to use them. Only adults were allowed to use aerial kicks, the officials said. Unless he stopped using them, Gavonnah could not compete.

If he wasn't going to be allowed to use his best moves, Gavonnah refused to compete. It was hard for Gavonnah, but he sat and watched the other kids compete in sixteen different events during the 2000 Florida Black Belt Association tournaments.

Then, later that year, Gavonnah heard some great news. The officials had spoken, and they had changed their minds.

They decided that aerial kicks were not dangerous for children to learn. Gavonnah and other children his age would be allowed to use aerial kicks in competitions, after all.

Gavonnah practices his moves with his older brother, Eli Thompson.

Gavonnah helps a young karate student.

Today Gavonnah watches other kids his age learn how to do fancy flips like his. Sometimes he even helps the other students. He feels proud. He knows that, because of him, children all over the world are being challenged to be the best that they can be.

CHAPTER FOUR

TALKING THE TALK

The final buzzer sounded. The Wizards, Washington, D.C.'s professional basketball team, had won the game. Twelve-year-old Grant Paulsen stood with a group of reporters, a microphone in his hand. Everyone was hoping to interview the Wizards' Michael Jordan, one of the all-time greatest basketball players.

Grant Paulsen

Michael Jordan in a basketball game against the Los Angeles Lakers.

Grant's hands started to sweat as Michael moved his way. He had interviewed sports legends before, but never someone as famous as Michael Jordan. When Michael looked in his direction, Grant lifted his microphone. He knew he had to ask his question quickly.

Grant's mouth felt dry. For a moment, his mind went blank. What were the words he had wanted to ask? Just as Michael started to turn away, Grant called out, "Michael, you had another sensational game! You shot twelve of twenty-two from the floor and scored thirty-four points! Did you get any added inspiration from your kids being here tonight?"

After Michael smiled, Grant felt relieved. He'd done it! He'd gotten his question out. Michael seemed to like the question. "It's always good to see your kids, even though they call you old!" Michael joked. "It was good hanging out with them today. I even got to watch them play a little bit. I felt very good all day, so I was able to come into the game loose. It was a big game, and somehow I found a rhythm early."

It was hard for Grant to imagine that he had just spoken with one of the most talented basketball players in the world. His heart was racing as he lowered his microphone back down and let another reporter ask a question. This was the moment he had always dreamed of.

Grant fell in love with sports when he was a small boy. His first love in sports was football. Grant and his mother used to watch all of the Washington Redskins' football games together. She loved the team and wanted Grant to be her "Redskins buddy." Grant quickly learned the numbers and names of the players.

Grant at the Baseball Hall of Fame

Grant began to watch sports whenever he was allowed. Morning, noon, and night, Grant flipped through the sports channels on his television. Before Grant was even in school, he had worn out the numbers on the remote control.

Once Grant started school, he imitated the **sportscasters** he watched. He became so good at conducting pretend interviews that he started to sound just like a real sportscaster.

Grant's uncle, a radio personality, suggested that Grant call the radio station during one of his shows. One afternoon Grant called and he was put on the air. Grant made predictions about who would win the upcoming weekend football games. His predictions turned out to be right!

Reporters from a local newspaper interviewed Grant about his radio **broadcasts**. They were so impressed with Grant's sports knowledge that they asked him to write a weekly article for their newspaper.

In 1999, Grant became part of the WUSA news team.

Word about Grant, the young boy sportscaster, traveled fast. WUSA TV9 in Washington, D.C., filmed Grant for a special news report. After Grant's report received a positive response from viewers, the station asked Grant to become part of their sports team. He appeared on their show once a week.

Grant interviews Jon Jansen of the
Washington Redskins.

Over the years, Grant has met many professional athletes and coaches. Having the chance to speak with some of these people makes Grant feel like he is one of the luckiest people in the world. Grant also gets to go to games for free. Sometimes he interviews athletes in their locker rooms.

Being a sportscaster is not easy. There are many things a good reporter must know how to do. Sportscasters need to have pleasant-sounding voices. They also need to know how to pace their words.

Grant poses with linebacker LeVar Arrington of the Washington Redskins.

A good sportscaster should never talk too quickly or too slowly.

Another important part of being a professional sportscaster is personality. No one wants to listen to a boring report. It's Grant's job to keep the listeners interested. That means he must keep his conversation lively.

Grant must also research the rules of sports, as well as individual players. He needs to make sure his facts are correct. If he made mistakes all the time, no one would trust him as a sports **authority** (uh-THOR-uh-tee).

Aside from being one of the youngest sportscasters in history, Grant lives a regular life. He goes to school and has lots of friends. He likes seeing movies and playing miniature golf.

Grant plans to go to college. Like the players he has met, Grant knows how to succeed. Grant may just become the best sportscaster out there. After all, he's already had plenty of experience!

**Grant stands on a stool to interview
Langston Walker of the Oakland Raiders.**

GLOSSARY

aerial (AIR-ee-uhl) taking place in the air

amputate to cut off or remove

authority (uh-THOR-uh-tee) someone who knows a lot about a subject

broadcast a television or radio program

disabled (diss-AY-buhld) not being able to do what you want to do because you are ill or injured in some way

dojo (DOH-joh) a school that gives training in self-defense

double amputee a person missing two limbs

gi (GEE) a traditional karate outfit

gymnast someone who does gymnastics

gymnastics (jim-NASS-tiks) exercises that are performed on special equipment

illegal against the rules

karate (kah-RAH-tee) a way of fighting that uses kicks and punches

official (uh-FISH-uhl) a person in sports who makes sure the rules are obeyed

Olympic Games a competition held every four years for athletes from all over the world

opponent someone who is on the opposite side

prediction a statement that tells what the future will bring

prosthesis (pross-THEE-siss) something that replaces a missing part of the body

Pterygium Syndrome a very rare condition that can result in many disorders of the body

Romania a country in southeast Europe

routine (roo-TEEN) a regular way of doing things

sportscaster a person who reports sports on television or radio

technique (tek-NEEK) a skillful way of doing something

triathlete (trye-ATH-leet) someone who takes part in a triathlon

triathlon (trye-ATH-lon) a race that has three parts, such as swimming, bicycling, and running

uneven bars a piece of gymnastic equipment made up of two parallel bars of different heights

FIND OUT MORE

Raising the Bar
http://www.nadiacomaneci.com
See over five decades worth of photos of Nadia Comaneci
and read her biography.

Proving Them Wrong
http://www.challengedathletes.org/caf/people.asp?id=50
Read more about Rudy Garcia-Tolsen's greatest competitive
highlights.

Changing the Rules
http://www.amazing-kids.org/akom11-02.htm#top
Check out Gavonnah William's trophies and read about his
accomplishments in karate.

Talking the Talk
http://www.kickoffmag.com/webexclusives/grant.shtml
Read one of Grant Paulsen's sports articles.

More Books to Read

For the Love of Karate by Rennay Craats,
Weigl Publishers, 2003

Letters to a Young Gymnast by Nadia Comaneci,
Basic Books, 2004

Top 10 Physically Challenged Athletes by Jeff Savage,
Enslow Publishers, Inc., 2000

Uncommon Champions: Fifteen Athletes Who Battled Back by
Marty Kaminsky, Boyds Mills Press, 2000

INDEX

PHOTO CREDITS

MEET THE AUTHOR

 Kirsten Hall has written more than sixty books for children. She has also taught preschool and elementary school. Spending time with kids has always been one of her favorite pastimes. She appreciates their fearlessness as they face a world filled with adult rules and expectations.

It is not surprising to Kirsten that so many kids have taken the world of sports by storm. Narrowing down her list of young athletes to the four who would be featured in this book was her biggest challenge. There are so many kids out there who are amazing athletes. She looks forward to writing about more of them.